Wa.

Amy Berryman is a New York-based writer and actor with roots in Washington State and West Texas. Her play *Walden* premiered in London's West End in 2021. Her other full-length plays include *The New Galileos*, *Three Year Summer*, *Epiphany* and *The Whole of You*. She has been a finalist for the O'Neill, NNPN's National New Play Festival, and for Shakespeare's New Contemporaries. Her work has been developed at theatres all across the US including TheaterWorks Hartford, Premiere Stages, People's Light, Bay Street Theater, Portland Stage, PROP Thtr, Samuel French OOB Festival, City Theatre, Kitchen Dog Theater, Landing Theatre, Caltech, Great Plains Theatre Conference, Valdez Theatre Conference, Nomad Theatricals, and AMiOS. The short film she wrote, co-produced, and starred in, *You Are Everywhere*, won Best Short Drama in the LA Short Film Festival 2018. As an actor, Berryman was seen off-Broadway in Jessica Dickey's *The Convent*, directed by Daniel Talbott with Rattlestick/Rising Phoenix Rep/Weathervane, as well as Greg Kotis's *Lunchtime* at the Brick, and Erin Courtney's *I Will Be Gone* in the Humana Festival. Proud member of Rising Phoenix Rep. amy-berryman.com

AMY BERRYMAN

Walden

faber

First published in 2021
by Faber and Faber Limited
74–77 Great Russell Street
London WC1B 3DA

Typeset by Brighton Gray
Printed and bound in the UK by CPI Group (Ltd), Croydon CR0 4YY

A CIP record for this book
is available from the British Library

978-0-571-37243-0

2 4 6 8 10 9 7 5 3 1

Walden had its world premiere at the Harold Pinter Theatre, London, on 22 May 2021. The cast, in alphabetical order, was as follows:

Stella Gemma Arterton
Bryan Fehinti Balogun
Cassie Lydia Wilson

Director Ian Rickson
Designer Rae Smith
Lighting Designer Azusa Ono
Sound Designer Emma Laxton
Composer Mark Bradshaw
Casting Director Amy Ball CDG
Assistant Director Sara Aniqah Malik

This production was presented in the West End by Sonia Friedman Productions as part of the RE:EMERGE Season, which was made possible with the support of Arts Council England.

Characters

Stella

early thirties, Cassie's twin sister.
Former NASA colony architect, her mouth moves quickly
to catch up with her even faster brain, her thoughts zigzag
like tracing a constellation. She is still deeply heartbroken
she will never go to space, harbors secrets and resentment
as she struggles to welcome her sister into her new life.
Born first.

Cassie

early thirties, Stella's twin sister.
NASA botanist, physically strong, seems put together in the
midst of all her success, but inside is doubtful and falling
apart. Overwhelmed by the deeply human experience she is
having since landing back on Earth. She digs and uproots.
Looking for a way to blow up her life, as well as looking
for a way to get closer to her sister.
Born second.

Bryan

mid-thirties, Stella's fiancé.
A member of the populist political movement Earth
Advocates, laid back, kind, emotionally open, strong, still
grieving the loss of his brother, struggling with the wall
Stella has built around herself.

When

The Not-So-Distant Future

Where

American Wilderness

WALDEN

'This whole earth which we inhabit is but a point in space. How far apart, think you, dwell the two most distant inhabitants of yonder star, the breadth of whose disk cannot be appreciated by our instruments? Why should I feel lonely? Is not our planet in the Milky Way?'

'Heaven is under our feet as well as over our heads.'

Henry David Thoreau, Walden

Notes

A '/' indicates overlapping dialogue.

Cassie and Stella should look like sisters and be of similar builds, but they need not look like identical twins. They look different, have different blood types, and have therefore always assumed themselves fraternal.

Consider what the future of America will look like when casting this play (reference the 2013 *National Geographic* article 'The Changing Face of America'). Bryan should be played by an actor of a different racial, ethnic, or cultural background than Cassie and Stella. The characters should reflect a more and more diverse America.

Act One

Darkness.
  Sounds of a shuttle landing. Cameras. Reporters. Commotion.
  And then, quiet. Lights come up on Bryan and Stella's home in the wilderness of America. It's a cabin, rustic, reminiscent of an earlier era. There are lush trees and mountains surrounding. There is a bottle of wine open, and a bottle unopened.
  Stella sits, waiting, touching her wine glass, her mind somewhere far away. Bryan enters.

Bryan Is she here?

Stella Soon.

Bryan nods, pours himself some wine. There's not much left in the bottle. He clocks this, sits with Stella.

Bryan Hey – cheers.

Stella half-heartedly joins him in a cheers.

You okay?

Stella nods, drinks another sip.
  After a moment, Bryan gets up, an idea hitting him with a sly smile.

You know what? (*As he goes.*) Basement!

He runs off, Stella looking up after him.

Stella What?

He doesn't answer her.
  Stella pauses a moment, downs the rest of her wine. One more glance at where Bryan departed, a glance at

the door, and she pulls out a slim device from her pocket. The screen brightens her face as she pulls up a news report, turning the volume down low.

Announcer . . . Thank you again to the Moon Habitat Team, we're so glad you're back home safe.

Turning now to update you on the tsunami, which some scientists are now referring to as a 'mega' tsunami that hit Sri Lanka three days ago – the number of missing persons presumed dead has climbed to almost one million. Yes, you are hearing that number correctly. Another ten thousand have attempted to seek refugee status in India, where they are not receiving much welcome due to the dire conditions involving the war over potable water. More from –

Stella hears movement from off and quickly shuts the device off and puts it in her pocket.
Bryan enters wearing a party hat, carrying a box of party materials. He blows into a noisemaker.

Stella . . . What are you doing?

Bryan I remembered – we had these in the basement!

Stella . . . it's not a birthday.

Bryan But it's a celebration! We can put them on, when she gets here.

Stella . . . No.

Bryan Why not?!

Stella Where did you even get those?

Bryan One time Michael threw me a surprise party.

Stella Oh . . .

Bryan I just thought . . .

Stella I think it's not . . . it's not like a party.
Can you put those away? I think she'll be here any minute.

Bryan Yeah I know. (*He takes the hat off.*) Are you okay?

Stella Yeah I'm fine, I'm . . .

Bryan It'll be good!

Stella I can't go online without seeing her face, and it's . . .

Bryan Ah.

Stella Every time I turn on the news . . . .

Bryan There's your first problem. Turning on the news.

Stella (*bristles at this, defensive*) I'm watching the news to hear about the tsunami, and of course that's not their lead story, it's the team back from the Moon . . . so I have to wait through that before I get to the *actual* news. The death toll is up to a million.

Bryan Jesus.

Stella They're saying all of Sri Lanka is off the map, and another ten thousand displaced people. India doesn't want anyone, obviously.

Bryan Uh huh.

Stella (*spiraling*) It's the worst possible timing, the worst place for it to happen, it's going to get worse, it's just going to keep getting worse, Pakistan keeps threatening them with nukes –

Bryan They aren't going to do that –

Stella Which would destroy the ozone, air quality is bad everywhere already, crops are completely fucked over there, it's just going to get worse, / a million is –

Bryan Hey. Hey.

Stella What?

Bryan Uh. Can we go back to the part about Cassie?

Stella . . . it's nothing. Never mind, I'm fine. Can you put those away, I'm going to grab the candlesticks.

She exits. Bryan observes her empty glass, and tries to pour some wine for her, but the bottle is empty. He goes to open the unopened bottle, a Volnay.

Bryan Can Cassie drink wine? I thought you said her body might be still off from being up there for so long . . . microgravity or – whaddaya-call – it – oh

The cork breaks.

Stell?

Stella comes back in, with candlesticks.

The cork broke.

This is the end of the world to Stella.

Stella Did you just –

Bryan I'm sorry –

Stella Why did you open that?

Bryan What? I was going to pour you more wine –

Stella You should have / asked me first

Bryan I didn't realize you were done with the whole bottle –

Stella I am in pain. I'm hurting.

Bryan I know.

Stella That took me two weeks to get that bottle, it's really rare, that's a real cork, it's old –

Bryan I'm sorry, I was just trying to help.

Stella You know cork trees are extinct, right? It's a really special bottle if it's got a cork in it, that's why I got this.

Stella finds an ugly old jar and sets it on the ground, grabs the bottle from Bryan. She sets some napkins on top of the jar, pushes the cork into the bottle and begins pouring it carefully through the napkin into the jar.

Bryan Is Cassie into wine, too?

Stella No, but
our dad was
I dunno
I didn't know what else to do.
It just seemed like the right thing to do.

Bryan Hey.
Tell me what you're feeling.

Stella (*not good*) I'm good.

Bryan Please talk to me. I hate . . .
I hate it when you do this

Stella Do what

Bryan You just stop talking. You don't tell me things. I'm trying to understand.

Bryan touches Stella – her body melts into his. They hold each other for a moment.

I know a lot has happened in the past week, I'm sad, I know we both are, and I can only imagine –

Stella They keep referring to her as James Ryan's daughter.

Bryan I see.

Stella Like, he has two daughters, he has twin daughters. I mean he had twin daughters.

Beat.

It's not a big deal, it's just sort of jarring –

Bryan It is a big deal –

Stella No it's fine, I'm just wondering . . . why I even invited her.

Bryan You were excited to see her, when you called her.

Stella That was before.

Bryan I know, but I'm so proud of you for taking this step . . . I think whatever happens, can only be good. Healing.

Stella I don't know if it can *only* be good . . .

Bryan And I get to meet her! This is the person who was in the womb with the woman I'm going to spend the rest of my life with! That is awesome.

Stella DON'T tell her we're getting married.

Bryan Oh – okay?

Stella And don't tell her you're an EA.

Bryan (*gesturing around the cabin*) Uh, she might figure that one out.

Stella Please don't tell her – I will tell her, I want to tell her. There's just a lot . . . there's a lot.

Bryan Yeah. Okay.

Stella We have to act really happy.

Bryan What? We are happy.

Stella Yeah yeah – *we* are happy – I mean we just have to act like, happy for her. You know?

Bryan . . . okay.

Stella I'm just going to change and – I'll be right back.

She exits. Bryan starts to put away the hats, but he puts one back on, fondly. Then there's a knock at the door, he turns, startled, forgetting about the hat.

Bryan Stell? She's here!

Bryan opens the door to reveal a bewildered Cassie, Stella's twin sister. She has a suitcase with her. She wears a blue mask over her mouth and nose, with a NASA symbol on it. Cassie takes off her mask, letting it hang around her neck, upon entering the house. Cassie is skeptical of everything around her, including Bryan.

Cassie Hi.

Bryan Hi!

Cassie Am I . . . in the right place?

Bryan I think so – you're Cassie!

Cassie Yes, I'm Cassie. Are you . . . Bryan?

Bryan Yep I'm Bryan!

Awkward beat as Cassie takes him in.

. . . You look great!

Beat.

I don't know if that's what you say to someone who just came back from space? But . . .

Cassie Uh. Thanks.

Bryan Thanks for coming all the way out here.

Cassie Yeah, it's . . . wilderness.

Bryan Yeah! We like it.

Cassie (*bewildered*) The air is so cool. It's cool outside.

Bryan Yeah. You know, you don't have to wear that.

Cassie (*touching her mask*) What? Oh, just a habit.

Bryan No really, within a hundred miles the air is totally safe. You don't need a mask.

17

Stella enters. The sisters see each other. They embrace before saying a word. It is both awkward and intense. Finally:

Cassie Hi.

Stella Hi.

Beat.

Stella You look

Cassie What

Stella The same.

They laugh.

Cassie Did you think my face would be . . .? (*She puffs out her cheeks like a chipmunk.*)

Stella I mean

Cassie Like Dad?

Stella Yeah.

Bryan What?

Stella Gravity pulls all the blood to the feet, so in space –

Cassie it doesn't, so when you come back, it makes the face look a little

Stella Our dad's did anyway when he came back from –

Cassie They kept showing some pictures of all of us side by side, at the event –

Stella Cassie, I'm sorry that I couldn't –

Cassie Oh, it's / okay.

Stella We just live so far out / here, and . . .

Cassie But they showed some pictures of me before I went up, and right after the descent, and I don't know, I think I do look a little different.

Stella Cassie this is Bryan.

Stella notices Bryan's hat and takes it off his head.

Bryan We met.

Cassie Yeah . . . we met.

Beat.

Bryan Stella says she's been seeing you all over the news!

Cassie Yeah . . . so many interviews. It's been exhausting.

Stella . . . Yeah, I bet.

Beat.

Can I take your bag?

Cassie Thanks, where am I – ?

Stella The couch. Uh – sorry the place isn't bigger . . .
There is a hotel um a few miles away, if that's better –

Cassie What? No, no. This is fine. It's *great*. I want to be with my sister.

Beat.

Stella Okay.

Cassie . . . I'm sorry I can't stay longer.

Stella That's okay –

Cassie Just have to get back.

Bryan Monday, right?

Cassie Yeah.

Stella For work?

Cassie Uh – yeah, just some, you know. Work.

Bryan More Moon Colony / stuff?

Stella Bryan /

Cassie . . . Habitat?

Stella shoots him a look, Cassie gives a little laugh, unsure how to respond.

Stella We've, um – we've cooked some food, you're probably hungry.

Bryan Deer! A deer I got. Stella said you'd eat deer?

Cassie *Deer?* . . . What . . . what do you mean?

Stella Deer have kind of invaded this area, it's so temperate, it has kind of become a problem. And we grow most of our own food.

Bryan Huge garden out back.

Stella We try to eat completely local. I've started eating meat again.

Cassie . . . wow.

Bryan How was the food in space?

Stella Bryan.

Bryan What?

Stella It's just – / that's not a good question.

Cassie Lella, it's / okay.

Bryan Lella?
What did you just call her?

Cassie Lella. It's what I've called Stella since – I don't know?

Stella Since we could talk. And I called her Pee.

Cassie That's what we called each other when we were little.

Bryan Pee?

Stella Dad kept trying to get me to say Cassiopeia.

Cassie Before he'd accepted that no one is going to actually go by the name Cassiopeia.

Bryan Cassiopeia.

Stella Yeah you know. The queen. The constellation.

Cassie rolls her eyes.

Cassie Anyway. Lella and Pee. That's what we called each other. When we were little.

Bryan I didn't know that.
Cute.

Cassie But the food! I mean, *it was a long year*. Everything tastes divine to me right now. I got all these 3D printed candies on the way here – do you want some? They don't have any sugar, only superfoods but they taste / amazing.

Bryan No, no we don't eat printed food.

Cassie You don't?

Stella I'll try one.

Cassie passes one to Stella. Bryan watches Stella chew the piece of candy. She shrugs at him.

So . . .
How do you feel?

Cassie Good. Really good. Fine. Happy. To be back.

Bryan I bet.

Cassie How are things here?

Stella Well, *here* they're good.

Bryan Oh, you know! The world's collapsing around us, but

Cassie God, I know. The bombs on Christmas? In India I mean? We could see them through one of our telescopes on the Moon. I guess the ISS could see it just from looking out the window.

Stella That must have been insane.

Bryan Stella's obsessed with the whole situation.

Stella Well we always knew it was coming.

Cassie Yeah, *that* many refugees, in a war zone, with no water . . . We've been calling it the PONR.

Stella frowns, trying to figure out what it could stand for.

Point of No Return.

Bryan Dramatic.

Stella NASA loves their acronyms.

Cassie (*she indicates her and Stella*) Makes our work, you know
It's just really important.

Beat.

Bryan (*as if to begin to disagree*) . . . Well –

Stella ANYWAY
Good things are happening too.

Cassie Yeah?
What things?

Stella and Bryan look at each other.

Stella Well, we're . . . we . . . are –

Stella struggles and Bryan makes a decision.

Bryan Getting married!

Stella BRYAN.

Cassie What?

Stella I TOLD you I wanted to / tell her.

Bryan What? I thought you *were* telling her –

Cassie Wait, what?

Bryan I was just –

Cassie What do you mean?

Stella What?

Cassie You're getting *married*?

Stella Yes.

Cassie Why?

Stella Cassie.

Cassie I'm sorry I'm just

Cassie and Stella communicate with their eyes.

I'm sorry Bryan, that was –
I have never known Stella to want to get married so
You are obviously a life-changing, amazing person!
This is – so great!

The mood has already been soured.

This is amazing! When will the wedding be?

Stella We haven't decided yet.

Bryan No rush.

Cassie Yeah no rush no rush.
I just, wow – Lella. I am so happy for you guys!

Stella . . . thanks.

Cassie When did this happen?

Bryan Couple months ago.

Cassie MONTHS ago?

Beat.

I guess I was thinking
    You could have told me
    You could have sent a message

Stella I

Cassie I mean I just learned of Bryan's existence when you called.

Bryan We weren't really telling a lot of people.

Cassie I would have loved to know that. Is all I mean.

Stella I didn't know how you would react.

Cassie What? I would have loved any good news, any contact from you.

Stella I just
    Couldn't.
    I'm sorry.

Beat.

Bryan Do you want some WINE?

He presents the ugly jar of wine.

Cassie That's wine?

Stella Long story, but yes that is a Volnay. In there.

Cassie No way. How'd you get that?

Stella Took a while, but I have ways.

Bryan pours them some wine.

Bryan So you can drink alcohol? Yet? Or?

Cassie Yes, I can drink.

Stella Do you feel any pain . . .?

Cassie You know what, my feet hurt a little, actually, and my sleep is a wreck
 but other than that . . .!

Stella Oh god, Dad's feet always hurt.

Cassie Yeah, I've been thinking about that.

Bryan His feet – ?

In the following, Stella and Cassie talk almost over each other, their sentences flowing together.

Cassie Well that was decades ago

Stella The third time our dad came back down from the ISS, after a year,
 his right leg – it didn't / break but

Cassie It was a fracture.

Stella Yeah.

Cassie His muscles were so weak from being up there for that long

Stella And Bart, his partner

Cassie Oh yeah – his legs did break

Stella BOTH of them

Cassie That was so awful

Stella When they got back

Cassie Thank god Dad

Stella Well he exercised more than Bart, up there, I guess

Cassie Yeah, that's what he always said

Stella But Dad's feet hurt – kind of for the rest of his life?

Cassie Well who knows how much of that / was him complaining

Stella Right, just

Cassie Or like reminding us

Stella Reminding us that James Ryan spent a year in space

Cassie Altogether, five years

Stella Right, all his missions added up: *five* years so –

Cassie (*rolling her eyes*) NASA's hero

   Bryan laughs.

Stella What?

Bryan Nothing, it's just
  It's funny to watch
  the sisters talk!

Stella What do you mean?

Bryan I've never seen you around each other.
  it's cool
  I see the twin-ness.

   Beat.

Cassie (*to Stella*) So, are you like into wine now?

Bryan She's really getting into it.

Stella Oh, I've just been learning a lot about it.

Cassie Ha, like Dad.
  So fancy.

Stella Not like Dad, I'm not
  Not a snob.
  The science is pretty fascinating.

Cassie Yeah? Tell me.

Stella Well, I've thought about you a lot, because soil is so much a part of it, like the vines where this wine comes from, in Burgundy, are grown primarily in Jurassic limestone –

Cassie Ohh, okay –

Stella (*gets very passionate*) – which makes it super unique, and there are so many different types – and each one varies in how difficult it makes the vines' ability to grow – it's really all about how hard the vines have to work, that can change the taste and tannins – the harder they have to work to grow through the limestone, the more complex the wine becomes . . . it's – *amazing*.

She beams and takes a sip.

Bryan I dunno, I'm a beer guy. Before I met Stella, I don't think I'd even tried wine that wasn't made down the way in somebody's basement.

Cassie attempts a laugh, shooting a look at Stella.

You should hear her talk about it at the bar.

Stella Bryan.

Cassie Bar?

Bryan She's been working at the bar in town.

Cassie does laugh now.

Cassie (*to Stella*) What? You're a NASA architect.

Stella I'm not. I'm not that. Anymore.

Beat.

Bryan Should we toast? Let's toast, I'd like to give a toast.

Cassie and Stella hesitate, and then hold up their glasses.

I'd like to toast the Moon. That it held Cassie safely for the past year so that she could return to Earth, intact, with the

strength to travel out to us. I'd like to toast the wine.
A beautiful thing too rare these days, grapes seeded in the ground, that fought their way into the light, and sacrificed themselves for our cups. I'd like to toast Stella, for saving me when I broke the cork of this wine, for saving me every day. And, finally, I'd like to toast the Earth. For hosting us, for continuing to give to us so freely when we take so much from her. May we give back to the Earth, every chance we can.

After a moment, Bryan raises his glass to signal he is done.

Cassie . . . cheers.

Stella Thank you, Bryan.

They 'cheers' and drink deeply. The toast, the taste of the wine, the cabin, the air all hit Cassie at once.

Cassie This is delicious.

Stella Isn't it?

Cassie . . . I kind of feel the need to wash my hands and maybe, like, my face.
Long drive.

Stella Oh sure, of course. Bathroom's down the hall.

Bryan You have to jiggle the handle when you flush.

Cassie I . . . What?

Bryan It's an old-fashioned toilet.

Stella (*rolling her eyes*) It's a fucking antique.

Bryan We're a little . . . old-fashioned around here.

Cassie Ha ha okay . . .

She exits.
Beat.

Stella Uh

Bryan What did she mean about the marriage stuff?

Stella I can't believe you did that –

Bryan (*shrug*) I thought that was the right moment –

Stella Don't tell her about

Bryan I won't, I won't.

   Beat.

I'm trying to be here for you and . . .

Stella And what?

Bryan You keep like
   scolding me.

Stella Scolding you?

Bryan You keep saying 'Bryan' in this way.

Stella I am not saying Bryan in any sort of way I'm just
saying your name.

Bryan Well
   That's not how it feels.

Stella (*not sorry*) Sorry.

Bryan It's that. It's that tone.

Stella Can you cut me a little bit of slack?

   She drinks more wine.

Bryan You can't even see how much slack I am cutting you.
   I'm trying to be sensitive.
   I'm just asking you not to take out what you're feeling
about your sister on me.

Stella I'm NOT.

   Cassie enters.

Cassie . . . that thing is like actually from the twentieth
century!

Bryan Hey, hey! But it works, right?

Cassie I guess.

Bryan Are you hungry? Getting hungry?

Cassie (*sensing tension*) Yes!

Bryan Great!
Why don't you two sit on the deck while I finish this up?

Neither woman immediately agrees.
Then:

Stella *and* **Cassie** Sure! Yeah okay.

Bryan Great! I'll be out in a bit.

Stella It's such a nice night.

Cassie It is.

Cassie and Stella find themselves the back deck. Sun will set in about an hour.
Soft, small animal sounds. Crickets. Birds.
The sisters are quiet for a while.

Engaged. Wow.

Stella Yeah. Sorry I didn't –

Cassie No, I'm sorry I acted so

Stella It's okay.

Cassie It's just
John
really wanted to marry you.

Stella I know.

Cassie You never wanted –
You said what's the point
that it's silly.

Stella I know.
　　Life is strange.

Cassie And this guy is . . .

Stella You don't know him.

Cassie Yeah, I definitely don't know him.

Stella . . . How is John?

Cassie Uh he
　　I don't know
　　We haven't really been speaking
　　he barely spoke to me
　　after it happened

Stella Oh

Cassie Everyone was upset
　　I think
　　Everyone misses you.

Stella . . . I see.

　　Beat.
　　　They look at the sky.

Cassie Where are your screens? I haven't seen any devices
or – ?

Stella (*deep breath*) Okay yeah so – Bryan isn't really into
technology.

Cassie Yeah, I got that vibe from the toilet.

Stella Sorry I wasn't able to give you . . . a heads-up about
this but – he's anti-cloning, anti-symbiotic embryo, anti-
synthetic foods . . .

Cassie Wow. He's like an Earth Advocate.

Stella Yeah. He is.

Cassie What?

Stella Yeah.

Cassie Are you serious?
  He's an EA?

Stella Yeah. Yes.

Cassie *What?*

Stella He doesn't judge me. For the work I used to do. And I don't judge him.

Cassie 'Work you used to do?'

Stella He thinks the government should be spending all that money on saving this planet, instead of looking for somewhere else to go –

Cassie And you know that it's *way* too late for that.

Stella I . . . it may be.

Cassie It *is*.

Stella Cassie, this is the border of Earth Advocate Community. It's growing, it's huge, and over the years . . . it seems crazy, but their impact seems to have made a difference. Even in the summers, it hasn't been over one hundred and ten degrees, ever, apparently.

Cassie That's because we are near mountains.

Stella A third of the country has stopped using electricity –

Cassie Earth Advocates don't make up a third of the country – ?

Stella Listen to what I'm saying – the people who live out here, there are so many people Cassie, *all kinds* of people, you wouldn't believe – they have cut their CO_2 emissions, collectively, on average, by eighty percent. EIGHTY. Sure, weather is complex, climate is complex, but the numbers don't lie. It's . . . I find it impressive.

Cassie . . . So EAs cut their emissions by, what, not using electricity?

Stella Yup, most don't use electricity at all.

Cassie But *you* are using electricity.

Stella (*smiling*) Yeah . . . it's a compromise. I can't live without the news, being online, being connected. We debate. We disagree. He has intelligent things to say about it. He's not blindly anti-science or anything.

Cassie Well so many of them are. We've stationed military units near the launch pad. There were thousands of protesters at the descent.

Stella Yeah.

Cassie I mean I've never even really talked to an EA?

Stella Well – now's your chance.
. . . He's a really good person.

Cassie Yeah. He seems great.
But you've only known him . . .

Stella I love him.
I've never felt this way.

Cassie You loved John.

Stella . . . I don't want to get into this.

Cassie Okay I'm just . . . trying to wrap my head around this.
I've been worried about you. I haven't known anything, about where you've been, what you've been doing, what your life is like now.
Are you doing okay?

Stella I'm okay. I'm good.

Cassie Good.
I know there's a lot to say but

Stella Cassie –

Cassie No just listen,
   I'm so sorry
   about what happened.

Stella You did what you had to do.

Cassie Lella –

Stella You did exactly what I would have done.

   Beat.

Cassie Yeah.

   Stella downs her wine, turns and heads towards the door.

Stella (*brightly, holding up her glass*) This is good though,
right?

Cassie Yeah. It's really good.

   Beat.

Stella I'm gonna go get some more wine, okay?

Cassie Okay . . .
   Stella.
   I'm really glad . . . really glad you asked me to come.

Stella (*barely turning around*) No, me too, it's great. Me
too.

   Transition.

Act Two

Late that night.

Cassie tiptoes out onto the deck with a glass of water.
She looks out into the darkness, listens to the crickets – then
hears someone stirring awake on a deck chair.

Cassie OH!

Bryan Oh uh what? Uh – oh. Shit. I was asleep. Hey. You
okay?

Cassie Sorry, I didn't see you –

Bryan No it's fine. I just dozed off. I was reading.

Cassie notices the book he is reading is Walden.

Cassie Stella making you read *Walden*?

Bryan What, you don't like *brilliant classic literature*?

Cassie . . . I sort of think it reads like a whiny hipster's blog
from nineteen-whatever.

Bryan Seriously? I find it pretty interesting.

Cassie I feel like she named it Walden just to annoy me.

Bryan Named what?

Cassie Her design. One of the missions she works – was
working on is named Walden. You didn't know that?

Bryan A NASA mission?

Cassie Yeah.
One of the Mars missions.

Bryan Ha.
Mars is hardly Walden Pond.

Cassie . . . Yeah.
Is Stella – ?

Bryan She's in bed, she goes to sleep earlier than me most nights. If it were up to me, we would both sleep outside, always.

Cassie . . . right.

Bryan Sit down. Join me.

Cassie Uh. Okay.

She sits, breathes in the air, again feeling very aware and alive, being out in the natural world for the first time in so long.

Bryan Isn't it great?

Cassie What?

Bryan The air out here.

Cassie Yeah . . . it is great. It's like a miracle.
I forgot what this feels like.
And all the sounds, the stars.

Bryan One of the only peaceful bits of the country left.

Cassie Ha, yeah. Maybe.

They sit. Cassie sips water.

Bryan So – you work with plants, right? Up there.

Cassie Uh, yeah. I work with plants and microorganisms. These tiny, microscopic – they're called extremophiles? They survive in extreme conditions. Like tardigrades and . . . a lot of my work is growing new kinds of vegetables, more nutrient-dense vegetables, in the greenhouses, but I also –
Maybe you saw this on the news –
Oh I guess you wouldn't have. I, uh –
One of my experiments was successful.

I achieved the first example of terraforming.
I made something grow
in the ground.

Bryan In the ground on the Moon?

Cassie Yeah.

Bryan For real?

Cassie Yeah. I still can't believe it. It's pretty huge.

Bryan So hold up. Not only did you walk on the Moon
every day for a year, but you made something *grow* there.
Holy shit. I am in awe of you.

Cassie Oh, thanks.
That uh
That surprises me.

Bryan What does?

Cassie With your – political stance?

Bryan Ah. She told you.

Cassie nods.

Look, you walked on the Moon. And *that* is awe-some.
Awe-worthy.

Cassie . . . Thank you.
THANK you.
It actually feels really good to hear someone say that.

Bryan Hasn't everyone been . . .?

Cassie Sure, yeah.
But.
. . . Not Stella.

Silence.

So a real live Earth Advocate just said my work is awe-
worthy. Wow.

Bryan Hey, now.

Cassie But – you use electricity . . .

Bryan I'm not that intense. I do as much as I can, but –

Cassie You guys have a car.

Bryan Yeah, a solar car.

Cassie That's what's so weird about EAs – you want to live in the past, but you also use the most advanced technology.

Bryan (*correcting her*) We use whatever's best for the planet. It's not about recreating the past, it's about working towards a future. The land has started to grow, animals are migrating back to this area, it seems to be making a difference.

Cassie Okay . . .

Bryan Look – we aren't against science, we aren't against NASA, we're just against colonizing. We should be saving our own planet, instead of colonizing another one.

Cassie Colonizing.

Bryan NASA announced the Moon Colony, right? That's what it was called. And then the EA movement put forth our demands: stop the plans, redirect the money, and we drew attention to the history of that word. We wanted you to stop. And you just…changed the word.

Cassie We aren't colonizing. We are fucking saving humanity. Maybe, *maybe* if the Earth Advocacy movement had grown to the size it is now like . . . fifty years ago, maybe. Maybe then there would have been time to turn this thing around, but now there isn't.

Bryan Maybe you missed what's been going on the past year, but the EA Communities now go from here all the way up to the Canadian border. More people are joining every day, young people, old people, genders, races, it's becoming more than just a movement, it's a force, I think it's creating real change.

Cassie And they were all protesting at my descent. Thousands of them.

Bryan Yeah, can you blame them? It's ridiculous – we're investing in this place light years away that we don't even know if our species can survive on –

Cassie The Moon isn't light years away.

Bryan Okay I didn't mean that literally.

Cassie Mars is about . . . 12.5 light *seconds* away.

Bryan Alright, you know what I mean.

Cassie We are investing in a place so far away so that in thirty, forty years we can still exist. We had the tools to do it decades ago and we didn't. Now we're running out of time.

Bryan No that's NOT what we should have done decades ago –

Cassie Here we are, at a precipice, our population is in grave danger, and the EA movement isn't what's going to save us, investing in a place far away is what will save us. And it's *the next step* – it's about innovation, it's about adventure, and learning –

Bryan Adventure? NASA finally was able to sucker our politicians into the palm of their hands, completely changed the course of our future, put all that money into 'habitation' – is that the word they want you to use? – put all that money into habitation when it could be spent – I don't know – solving the water crisis in India? But no, let's colonize for the 'adventure' of it – are you kidding me?

Cassie No, that's not what I meant –

Bryan There's life on Mars, anyway, isn't there? There's water –

Cassie There's water, yeah –

Bryan So we're just going to go put our shit there, take it over, no regard for any life that's already there. Sounds familiar, doesn't it?

Cassie Stella says it better than me.
Hasn't she ever talked to you about this?

Bryan Oh she's told me things. She's told me some of the crazy stuff they make you do.

Cassie Like what?

Bryan Forced vasectomies? Birth control implants when you were, what, sixteen?

Cassie It's not forced, at all. We committed our lives to exploration, to science, even that young, yeah, we made the choice. You make that choice, you aren't going to have kids, it's just not what we do. But it is reversible, anyway, all of it.

Bryan shakes his head a bit, decides not to go there.

Bryan Well . . . she seems really traumatized by all of it. It honestly takes a lot for me to get anything out of her about NASA. When we met, in therapy, she talked about it, at length, but once we got together –

Cassie You met in *therapy*?

Bryan Group therapy, yeah. She didn't – ? I guess when would she have told you.

Cassie I'm
That's good she was in therapy.
Why were *you* in therapy?

Beat.

Sorry, that's a really personal

Bryan I lost my brother. We were driving up in the mountains and there was ice and I hit a tree.

Cassie Oh, god.

Bryan He was in the passenger seat.

Cassie I'm so sorry.

Bryan So Stella and I bonded over that.

Beat.

Cassie Wow. Yeah. Over the loss of a sibling?

Bryan Yeah.

Cassie (*sarcastic*) So did I . . . die?

Bryan Come on. It was still a loss. We both lost something.

Cassie She could have just called me up on the satellite.

Bryan You get what I'm saying, right? That this has been hard?

Cassie I know.

Bryan She lost out. On a lifelong dream. And she watched her twin sister live it.

Cassie I didn't even want it. I didn't even really want it.

Bryan Come on. You must have wanted it.

Cassie No.

Bryan It takes a lot of effort to do what you did.

Cassie Yeah. It does.
    What I mean is I've always loved space because Stella loves space. I followed Stella to space camp, I followed her everywhere . . .
    Botany is kind of my own thing, but NASA and science and ambition . . . that's not really me. It is me, but it's me because of Stella.

Bryan I see.

Cassie I mean, and our dad. And all that.

Bryan Nepotism.

Cassie (*smiles*) Whoaaa. Whoa. / The man calls it like it is.

Bryan (*also smiling*) I'm sorry.

Cassie No, it's funny. It's . . . it's *true*.

They both laugh.

Bryan . . . Do you want a drink or something?

Beat.

Cassie Yeah. Yeah, sure.

Bryan Cool.

He gets up, goes to kitchen.

Beer?

Cassie Beer sounds good.

Bryan Okay – no pressure but – I have two kinds. I have a nice six-pack from a place down the road and then . . . I also have my own? Brew?

Cassie Of course you do.

Bryan Yeah I knew you wouldn't want to –

Cassie No no, let's see the Bryan Brew.

Bryan Bryan Brew! That's what I call it!

Cassie No shit.

Bryan (*coming back out with the beers*) Stella doesn't really like beer.

Cassie But she's all into wine now, I guess?

They share a moment of 'what the fuck ever'.

Bryan Hey, whatever makes her happy, you know? I like making her happy.

Cassie . . . That's good.

Beat.

Cassie Is she happy?

Bryan I think so.

Cassie Really? Out here? *Bartending?*

Bryan Like I said, I think she . . . is.

Cassie I think she should come back to work for us. She's fucking brilliant. We need her. There's so much she could do. That's all based here on the ground.

Bryan Yeah.
You can lead a horse to water.

Cassie What?

Bryan You can lead a horse to water, but you can't make it drink?

Cassie Oh.

Bryan It's just an old saying.
My brother always used to say shit like that.

Cassie Yeah? What was his name?

Bryan . . . Michael.

Cassie Michael.
When was it . . . ?

Bryan What?

Cassie When he

Bryan The accident? Uhh a little over a year. Ago.

Cassie Oh. Recent.

Bryan Yeah.

Cassie What was he like? Was he an EA?

Bryan Hardcore. He's who got me into it.

Cassie Oh really?

Bryan No electricity. Didn't like driving. Hated my car, I used to have a truck. Vegetarian.

Lived way up in the mountains, with a bunch of hardcore EAs. He would lay into me about my hunting, always. Go on and on about how much water it takes to process meat. How it would take gallons and gallons of water to process one burger that's sold at a restaurant, stuff like that.

Beat.

Cassie And you were in the car.

Bryan I was driving, yeah.

Cassie You survived.

Bryan Yeah.

Cassie That sucks, right? That sucks.

Bryan laughs.

Bryan Exactly. Exactly! It sucks. It's the worst! I survived. Dark humor. I like it.

Cassie I get that. I really get that.

Bryan Yeah. Yeah . . . It was just a mistake.

Beat.

After it happened, I got the solar car. It's safe. It's really safe. Safest car.

Beat.

So the way I see it?
    Stella's lucky.
    You're right. You didn't die.
    She gets hers back.

Quiet.

They look at each other, see each other. Then Bryan shifts, gets up.

What's the next step for the Moon colony?

Cassie laughs despite herself at his word choice, realizing this guy is going to keep giving her shit. He laughs too.

Cassie The Moon *habitat*? The plan is to send the first group in six months.

Bryan It's expensive as fuck to be one of the first, right?

Cassie Yeah.

Bryan A couple million or something?

Cassie Try a billion?

Bryan So it's just the one percent who get to be saved by the great NASA.

Cassie Come ON –

Bryan Just the one percent – or maybe the zero point zero-zero-one percent – who you know are contributing the *most emissions*, their families get to be saved by NASA –

Cassie It's a process, there's the lottery –

Bryan Fucking lottery, right, right. A few of us plebeians might get anointed.

Cassie The plan is to move to the lottery model, it's just . . . Being one of the first. Yeah, it costs money.

Bryan You know what, I'm just gonna take a big sip of my beer every time I want to talk politics.

Cassie No it's okay, say whatever you want, I'm . . . I hear you.

Bryan I mean, let's be honest – the Moon is a rock, right? It's just a rock.

Cassie It could be argued that the Earth was once just a rock.

Bryan Right, but –
 What we have is all here. You can see it – out here,
tonight. Look. Look at that evergreen. Look at the vines
around the deck. Listen. Listen to the sounds.

> *They listen and look.*

I hate the cities. All that concrete and marble and glass –
you forget where you are. It feels like a different Earth out
here, right? That's why I live out here, I want to breathe it,
I want to feel it, I don't want it to be muted by billboards
and lights and all that manmade shit. When you put your
hands in dirt and earth, or feel branches snap under your
feet – I just think that's what we're meant for. This is what
we're meant for. Here. This is where we were born. Do you
feel – human? On the Moon?

> *Cassie feels overwhelmed by everything she is feeling, she
> can't help but admit this truth:*

Cassie No.
 I felt purposeful. I felt sharp.
 I felt strong.
 But
 I didn't feel like this.
 I forgot what it was like
 to feel like . . .
 To have a drink.
 To talk like this.
 Out here.
 I don't want to not feel . . .
 I wonder
 if *this* is what I want.

Bryan What?

Cassie This.

They are looking at each other, connected, and a little confused.

Stella (*from off*) Bryan?

She stumbles in. They part.

What are you doing?

Cassie Hey, / Lella.

Bryan Couldn't sleep.

Stella Can you come to bed?

Beat.

Bryan Yeah sure. I'll be right there.

Stella stumbles back to bed.

Goodnight.

Cassie Night.

Transition.

Act Three

Afternoon the next day. Sun is still out. Stella and Cassie in front of the house, a little breathless after a hike, in the middle of an argument over a childhood story. Even in the midst of the argument, they look super happy after being in the sun – they are calling off to Bryan, who is not far behind them.

Cassie So Stella named every rock in this rock collection and named them after her favorite literary characters. She was twelve. She had already read all of Le Guin, and Tolkien, and / Octavia Butler –

Stella And you stole them –

Cassie I didn't steal them –

Stella The point is that Gollum and Lavinia and Lauren – my rocks – were stolen by someone –

Cassie I did not steal them, I borrowed them and I did experiments on them –

Stella Borrowed? You hid them from me!

Cassie I liked them. I like rocks, I like soil, it's not my fault!

Bryan enters, small potatoes in his arms. He tosses one to Cassie, who barely catches it.

Bryan These are gonna be the best potatoes you've ever had. They don't need anything, don't even need butter. Trust me. Just wait.

Cassie Okay. It is a really nice garden you've got, it's huge. I didn't realize.

They look out at the garden.

Bryan The soil used to be dead. Used to be nothing, but past few years it's all I've been focused on.

Stella He's very proud.

Bryan (*a bit teasing*) You don't need to print food when you can grow it.

Cassie (*a bit teasing back*) Well some aren't so lucky, Bryan. Not everyone can grow their own food.

Bryan Maybe if the government gave everyone the means with which . . .

Cassie There are such things as food deserts.

Bryan But you grew something from nothing. Up there. Right?

Cassie nods. Stella looks between them: Bryan didn't know that yesterday.

Why can't we do that here?

Cassie It's a good question, and I talked about that in some of the interviews – I think now that it's happened, I think we can –

Stella I'm going to go get some wine. Anyone else? Bryan, beer?

She goes. Bryan and Cassie look at each other. They follow Stella into the house.
Inside, Stella opens a bottle of wine. A brief silent moment, then:

Cassie But anyway – Bryan, so, Stella is a nerd, she likes to collect weird things and name them.

Bryan She does like naming things. She calls the garden Middle Earth, did she tell you that?

Cassie cracks up.

Cassie Classic.

Stella I resent this conversation and I am very good at naming things.

Cassie You are terrible at naming things!

Stella Oh my god – she always says this –

Cassie I was telling him about Walden.

Stella Oh.

Slight beat as Stella recovers from this surprise.

Bryan You never told me you named something Walden.

Stella Yeah . . . well our dad –

Cassie It's just Dad's favorite thing of all time. He had most of the book memorized.

Cassie The 'Solitude' chapter –

Stella He read it, his first mission, when he was up there by himself for a year? Over and over again. He would quote it at us. Do you remember?

Cassie Oh yeah.

Stella Like . . . 'This whole earth / which we –'

Cassie *(Dad impression)* '– Which we inhabit is but a point in space. How far apart, think you, are the two most – *(Trying to remember, Stella helps her a bit.)* distant inhabitants of yonder star, the breadth of whose distance cannot be measured by our instruments?'

Stella laughs and adds to the Dad impression.

Cassie *and* **Stella** 'Why should I feel lonely? Is not our planet in the Milky Way?'

They laugh.

Bryan I like that.

Stella Like, when he would go up, and we would be sad. Or if . . . we were missing each other, or, feeling . . .

Cassie Lonely.

Stella His point being we are never alone.

Slight scoff from Cassie.

Yeah, so . . . a Mars habitat, I mean given how integral nature is to the design, I thought Walden felt . . . right.

Cassie Has Bryan seen the design?

Bryan Nooooo. He *hasn't*.

Cassie We can pull it up on a screen.

Sudden tension between Bryan and Stella.

Stella No –

Cassie Why not?

Stella I'll just – I can just tell him about it.

During the above, Bryan grabs a beer, Stella begins opening a bottle of wine. She demonstrates with the bottle.

So okay, Walden – It's a cylinder shape, which is the best shape to survive Mars' windstorms . . . And everything inside is based on bio-regenerative life support systems.

Cassie So there are plants everywhere –

Bryan And that's . . .?

Stella It's a way for us to use renewable energy from plant life – essentially creating our own eco-system – the plants supply us the oxygen and get rid of the CO_2 in the air, we use our waste and water to give back to the plants . . .

Bryan Whoa.

Stella The plants feed us . . . it's like a circle.

Cassie She incorporated it into every detail.

Stella Yeah, so it's all sustainable and . . . yeah.

Bryan That sounds amazing. So cool.

Cassie And it's beautiful, there's this gradient pattern on the HDPE level – can't we pull up the plans on a screen and show him? The virtual tour?

Stella No no no – it's fine. He gets it.

Cassie Why not?

Stella Just . . .

Bryan I don't use screens.

Cassie Bryan, you won't look at her brilliant work?

Stella It's fine.

Cassie Sorry but I think that's really messed up.

Stella Cassie, just drop it.

Cassie I don't get this. I don't think you not looking at your fiancé's work is going to save the planet.

Stella Cassie?

Bryan It's my choice, and Stella accepts me.

Cassie Can you imagine what Dad would be saying now?

Stella What, you've never questioned Dad? You never questioned whether this was the right move?

Cassie What do you even mean? We are already way further along than anyone predicted.

Stella I know.

Cassie I know you know.

Stella It's just, when you look at the money, the trillions being spent on colonizing –

Cassie It's too late to turn things around!

Stella We could use that money to help people. Alleviate suffering. Putting money towards solving the refugee crisis.

Cassie But we need another option, we need to take the next step, you are the one who always used to say that. This is –

Bryan Okay let's –

Cassie *Bullshit.*

Bryan Drop it.

    Beat.

Let me help you, Cassie. Let me tell you what I say to Stella. (*To Stella.*) I love you. I disagree with you! And I love you.

Stella I love you too.

    Silence.

Bryan I at least lead a pretty good hike, right?

Cassie That was . . . yeah. Beautiful. And to be out in it without even a mask . . . that was . . .

Bryan You see why we like it out here, right?

Cassie Yeah.

Bryan Listen, I'm starving, I think I'm gonna go check the traps? Kind of sick of deer, ya know?

Stella Okay.

Bryan Also, I think it might rain? My knee's acting up.

Stella You always say that, it's not gonna rain.

Bryan I might be right this time!

They kiss, Stella pulls him back in for a longer one.
A slightly awkward moment. He leaves.
    A little silence.

Cassie I like him, Lella. I like him. I actually like an EA.
He's so great . . .
    But you get that he is wrong, right?
    I get that you're trying to see his side, but –

Rain is heard.

Stella (*changing the subject*) Oh my god he was right, that
asshole.
    Ha, he's gonna get rained on . . .

Cassie . . . That lake was BEAUTIFUL. And so close! Do
you swim there?

Stella Oh, no. I haven't been swimming.

Cassie . . . what? You used to swim twice a day.

Stella I did it to build up strength. For simulations and tests.
    So I stopped.

Cassie What? You're such a good swimmer. You love
swimming.

Stella I mean I'd just always done it, it's what Dad said
would help me the most, and so I just always did it. But
yeah, that's something I've realized since I moved out here
and started, just, living, you know, differently.

    Beat.

It was awful, what happened, but in some ways, it's been
good. (*Takes a big gulp.*) I don't have to swim anymore.

Cassie Well, that's good. That's good.

    Beat. Stella drinks.

Cassie But . . . bartending? Really?

Stella I actually *love* it. I just wanted something different.
I wanted to work with like – normal people. Who aren't
fucking scientists and the most fucking brilliant humans
who've ever lived. These people are just so easygoing but
also SMART, you know? I guess I always thought regular
folks aren't that smart.

Cassie They aren't, really.

Stella Shut up.

Cassie I'm kidding, I'm kidding.

Stella But I used to think that. You know? I really did.
I used to think – never mind.

Cassie No, what? Tell me.

Stella I used to think if you weren't working on the kind of
work we do – that I did – that you weren't doing anything
to further the good of the human race, like, Jesus, I was on
such a fucking high horse, even when I first moved out here,
like I love Bryan, but I was like, 'Why does he live out here?
What do people DO out here?' You know? And I guess I've
started to see how nice it is to just live a quiet life. Garden.
Love someone.

Cassie Yeah. Sure. That's. Yeah.

Stella What do you think?

Cassie (*she means it*) I think
    Honestly? I think it's a nice thought.

Stella (*a little touched*) Thanks. Yeah.
    . . . Dad wouldn't have thought so.

Cassie NOPE.

They laugh.

Dad would have come out here – oh my god – if he'd have seen this place.

Stella Oh my god, and I haven't told you about the generator, it's such a piece of shit –

Cassie Oh that would have been the first thing he wanted to see –

Stella I KNOW. He would have had a panic attack.

Cassie And THE TOILET?

Stella OH my god. The toilet.

Cassie 'STELLA. WHAT THE HELL IS THIS?'

Stella Like when I got a B in English in high school.

Cassie Oh god

Stella 'NO DAUGHTER OF MINE'

Cassie 'No daughter of mine.'

Stella I was like, 'Dad! I got all A's in chem and physics, what more do you want from me?!'

Cassie Obviously perfection.

Stella What a fucker.

Cassie Yeah.

Stella I miss him.

Cassie Me too.

> *Beat.*
> *Thunder.*

Stella Shit.

> *They listen to the storm for a moment.*

Cassie Remember when it stormed during the simulation?

Stella Mars? In Hawaii?

Cassie No, no the big storm. The Moon / simulation.
In Nevada.

Stella Oh my god, yeah that lightning was –

Cassie And Lieutenant Roscoe was scared out of his mind –

Stella Oh yeah I completely forgot that.

Cassie (*laughing*) He was giving us that speech about
resilience and then the lightning struck, like, right behind
him –

Stella (*laughing*) His scream –

Cassie Yeah

Stella That was hilarious.

Their laughter dies down and a sadness hangs in the air.

Stella How's *he* doing?

Cassie Lieutenant?

Stella Yeah.

Cassie Good. I mean he's still a dick.

*There is a long, long silence here where Stella gets up and
pours herself more wine. Cassie is trying to figure out
what to say.*

He wouldn't tell me anything, so I refused to speak to him.
I would just nod or shake my head. I wouldn't even say yes
sir or no sir. All he would tell me is you were no longer part
of the mission. And then he told me – did he tell you this?

He told me that in the DNA test, they found out we're
identical. Which is insane.

Stella Yeah. Yeah he told me that.

Cassie Dad never thought to get that tested?

Stella We have different blood types. Most of the time that means you're fraternal.

Beat.

Cassie I was worried you had something, some heart thing, like Dad.

Stella No, no. It was nothing like that. It was just . . . They didn't want to give me another chance. After I didn't do well with the Gs in the centrifuge, and the bari chamber –

Cassie Right

Stella And then when I blacked out in the swimming test, I guess . . . yeah.
He just said
I wasn't fit
to go up
ever
that I'm never going to be an astronaut
it's too much of a risk and
when I asked for one more chance he said
No, *but*
he said
He said that because
we're actually identical,
I could be the control.
For how microgravity effects *your* body

Cassie Yeah

Stella And
I just
I don't know
I just wanted out of there.

Cassie And you just left. You didn't even say goodbye. I just was really in the dark. And so was John.

Stella I sent John an email.

Cassie (*bitter*) Yeah. You sent John an email. Eight years and that's all you gave him.
   And me . . . I don't even get an email.

Beat.

Stella Cassie, look, I didn't –

Cassie Would you ever
   consider
   coming back? To
   do tests?
   To be the control?
   I did tests every day.
   I did them in case you would . . . be willing.
   So it could be good, if you would come.

Stella They already have my blood, they have samples.

Cassie Right but, if they needed more.

Stella Why would they need more?

Cassie It would be really valuable
   information
   to have because

Stella Wait

      . . .
   wait.

They look at each other.

Cassie It's not

Stella Why did you come here?

Cassie To see you. NOT –
   look.

Stella Wait.

Cassie I'm not exactly sure how to say this.
   So I'm just going to say it.

They want me to lead Walden.
And
I don't know what to do.

Beat.

I would start training Monday. It's very preliminary training . . . wouldn't go up till next year. Still twenty people. I'd lead the scientific base.

Stella Walden is happening?

Cassie Yes.
The war, the refugee crisis, and then my . . . the breakthrough . . . it's moving the plans forward.

Stella How . . .
(*She can't help but briefly smile.*) Wow. They chose Walden. And . . . has the design changed?

Cassie I mean, I think John has made a few tweaks, but as far as I can tell it's still yours.

Stella John is going?

Cassie Of course. He has to. He's who knows the design.
They want me to ask you.
Offer you.
Hold on.

She goes to her bag and gets a manila envelope. Places it in front of Stella.

This is an offer. An official job offer. For you. To be a part of the team on the ground.

Stella Even though I left like I did?

Cassie Yes! They need you.

Stella Really?

Cassie Yes! Look in the envelope, it's all there. They wouldn't have asked if they didn't want you, you know them. You'd manage the mission from the ground, and they'd run weekly tests on your body so we can compare our DNA once I'm there.

Stella Weekly.

Cassie That's their proposal.

Stella What, forever?

Cassie It's their best shot at testing the long-term effects on the human body.

Stella So that's why you're here.

Cassie I'm here to see you. Because you asked me to come. And yeah, to offer you this. To ask you. They thought it would be better if I was the one to . . .

Stella No.

Cassie Please.

Stella No. You don't get it. I am done. I'm done.

Cassie I don't understand. If I hadn't passed the tests, I would still absolutely work in the field, I would assist from the ground, I would do it. It's – I mean I feel like I learned from you, that it's a duty.

Stella You would work from the ground, but you aren't sure if you'll accept the mission?

Cassie It's a really complicated – decision.

Stella No it's not – You should go. You have to go. You've been asked. You want to talk about *duty*?

Cassie It's – I know –

Stella Isn't this the goal? This is the highest goal.

Cassie Well I guess I'm not thinking about it like a 'goal'
    I'm thinking about it being for the rest of my life.
    I never imagined this.

Stella What are you talking about? We always imagined this.

Cassie It's something I never imagined happening alone.

Stella You won't be alone.

Cassie *Without you.* I mean without you.
  Lella, we are talking about the rest of my life.
  You'll never see me again.
  and you won't even –
  all you can say is
  you should go.

Stella You should.

  Beat.

Cassie I thought you might acknowledge – the sacrifice.
I would be making. I don't think it will be much of a life.

Stella Any person who is asked to do this and decides not
to do it is a person I truly don't understand. And to *lead* the
base? (*She kind of laughs.*) You can't say no. You can't. For
me it would not be a choice.

Cassie Really?

Stella Yes. Even now, now that I'm with Bryan, and have
built a life here, if I was given that opportunity, it wouldn't
even be a choice for me. THAT is a duty.

Cassie So it's a duty for me to go. Isn't it a duty to help me?
To help us? There's so much we can learn about the human
body out there, if they can test –

Stella I – I am done. I don't want to go back there. They
mistreated me, they were assholes to me –

Cassie They didn't mistreat you, you failed.

  Beat.

Stella So that's what you think.

Cassie . . . I don't know what I think.

Stella It's not my fault. It's not my fault I got the body I got.

Cassie Hardly anyone's body can do what we do –

Stella Nope, just yours I guess. Just the body that SHOULD be the same as mine. My *identical* twin.

Cassie I knew they shouldn't have tested us together, I knew it would mess with your head.

Stella You don't get it. My body is broken. I hate my stupid body. I hate it. It won't do anything. My whole life I've been trying to make it work. Do what I want it to do. And now I've met someone, that I look at I am, like, wow I want to raise a human with him, I want to have a baby, and it won't do that either.

Cassie What?

Stella I think it's broken.
I was going to tell you
You were going to come and I was going to tell you
That I'm having a baby
And now it's just gone
It's gone

Cassie What? When?

Stella And it makes me think
of our mom
and I wonder, I guess I wonder . . .

Cassie When was this?

Stella It just happened. A little over
A little over a week ago.

Cassie Oh my god are you okay?

Stella No. No. I am not really okay.

Cassie You wanted a baby?

Stella I did. I did want it.

Cassie We've never wanted . . .

Stella I know I know
But I wanted it, I wanted it.
Everything hurts.

Cassie I don't know what to say.
I would
I would give it all to you if I could
I don't even know if I want any of this

Stella Give all what to me?

Cassie Everything. You know. My body, the Moon –

Stella Oh my god don't say that
Do you hear yourself?

Cassie I wish that I could –

Stella YOU DON'T GET TO GIVE THOSE THINGS TO ME

Cassie I know, but I want to –

Stella I can't do this. I can't do this.

Bryan enters carrying several dead rabbits from the traps.

I need the key.

Bryan Key?

Stella To the car.

Bryan What? Why?

Stella I need to get out of here.

Bryan Wait a few minutes, I'll come with you –

Stella No, I need to
I need to be alone.

Bryan looks between them.

KEY. PLEASE.

Bryan I'm not giving you the key, you've been drinking.

Stella Fine. I'll walk.

Bryan Wait –

Stella leaves. Bryan runs out after her, leaving the dead rabbits on the table. Cassie looks at them as she can hear muffled yelling outside.
Bryan enters again, angry.

Cassie Where's she going?

Bryan I don't know, there's no point in going after her when she's like this.
What the hell happened?

Cassie We had a fight . . .
I've been asked to go on a mission to Mars
and I told her that and it sort of opened up
a bunch of . . .

Bryan (*a little lost/trying to process/still pissed*) Wait so what?
I . . . can't believe this is a conversation I'm having with a person.
That you're going to go to MARS.
What the fuck.

Cassie I'd be inhabiting the scientific base that was built by the last team that went.

Bryan The team that –

Cassie Yes. And we would build a habitat. Her design. Similar to what we just did on the Moon, but – I'd be there for – (*She laughs a little at the absurdity.*) the rest of my life.
And the first thing she said was
'You should go'

Bryan I see.

Cassie And JOHN is going.

Bryan Who's John?

Cassie John? *John* John? . . . He's an engineer who worked on Walden with her, and they . . .

Bryan OH that guy. Yeah. I forgot his name.

Cassie She's told you about him, right?

Bryan Yeah, a bit, but I don't care about stuff like that.

Cassie Well, I'd be going with him. I'm sure it's hard to hear.
  I don't know how much she's told you
  about how much she wanted this sort of thing to happen
to her?
  She devoted her life up to this point to exploration
  and we thought we would do it together, you know?
  Maybe even with our dad?
  But of course then he died, and . . .
  I don't know if I'm explaining this well.

Bryan Hey you have like a device, right?

Cassie . . . yeah.

Bryan Maybe could I use it?

Cassie (*handing hers over*) You don't even have . . . ?

  He texts on the device. Waits. Storm sounds.

Bryan She's just had a tough time lately.

Cassie Yeah
  that came out, too.
  That she
  that you – that she lost?
  A baby?

Bryan . . . yeah
Yeah it really freaked her out.
Your mom died having you, right?

Cassie Yeah, she did.

Bryan I told her it's probably not about that, I mean . . .
but . . . I don't know.

Cassie Stella has never wanted kids.

Bryan Well, she wants them, now.

Cassie We both have always thought bringing a baby into
the current world is a really stupid idea.

He gets a text.

Bryan Oh hey – (*Reads quickly.*) 'Went to the lake. Be back
later.'
. . .
'Went to the lake'? It's fucking storming, what
That's it? Just 'Be back later.' That's all I get?
(*Yelling at the device.*) That's all I get?!

*He makes to throw it. Thinks better of it, throws
something else.*

(*Still yelling.*) Sorry.

Cassie It's okay.

Bryan She doesn't TALK. I'm not.
I don't know, I'm not like that.
I need to talk when I'm upset.
I need to throw shit.

Cassie Yeah. Me too.

Bryan kind of roars.

She's always been like that.
Clams up when she's upset.

Bryan It took so long for her to really let me in.

Cassie Yeah.

Bryan That's not how relationships WORK.
You have to TALK.
You can't just – sense.
I can't *sense*. I don't know how to help her anymore!

Cassie Me either.

Bryan sighs and turns his attention to the potatoes and rabbit – begins to clear space, chop a few potatoes.

Bryan When would this happen?

Cassie What?

Bryan Mars.

Cassie Next year. But – prelim training starts Monday.

Bryan Ho-ly shit.

Cassie Yeah.

Bryan And you don't want to go?

Cassie I don't know. Of course, I've always wanted . . .
There are hundreds of astronauts in line behind me to take my place if I say no. You have no idea how many people want this. This is like . . . it's like an athlete qualifying for the Olympics. Or it's Everest . . . it's the Big One. For us.

Bryan Even after everyone on the first Mars mission died?

Cassie Yes. We're all a little nuts. We want to know what's out there.

Bryan (*problem solving*) Well, okay – How long will it take you to get there?

Cassie It would take a little less than nine months.

Bryan Fuuuck. So wait.

Doesn't that mean you could potentially come back?

The first mission to Mars, weren't they going to come back? And that's how . . .?

Cassie I mean, yes, technically, Mars' atmosphere can create methane, yeah, we could. But.

You saw how well it worked last time. That's why it's taken so long for us to go again.

Bryan Yeah.

Cassie The plan is to stay.

Bryan Who else would go with you? How many?

Cassie Twenty to begin with.

Bryan Twenty!

Cassie Yeah.

Bryan Hope you like them.

Cassie Ha ha, yeah.

Bryan . . . Is there anyone?

Cassie Anyone what?

Bryan You know. That you like.

Cassie Oh. No.

Bryan What about on the Moon?!

Cassie What about it?

Bryan You have, like – a Moon . . . person?

Cassie I was just there for a year. *Working.*

Bryan Right, and other people were there.

Cassie Yeah.

Bryan Did you fall in love ON THE MOON?

Cassie laughs.

How epic would that be?

Cassie Pretty epic.
But no. I didn't.
I haven't . . . had anything like that for a while.
A long time.

Bryan Well do you want something like that?

Cassie There's no point in wanting something
when you aren't going to have it.

Bryan What do you mean?

Cassie I'm going to go to Mars.
That's not the kind of life I'm
supposed to have I guess.

Bryan But you don't have to go.

Cassie Right. But I should.

Bryan Why do you want to go?

Cassie I want to go because . . .
I'm the best person for the job.
I am the one who should go.

Bryan But forget should.
Why do you *want* to go?

Cassie I don't think I do want to.

Bryan Well, there's your answer.

Cassie It's not that simple.

Bryan So why *don't* you want to go?

Cassie Because I . . .
I'm feeling like I want a life?

I want to really live?
But it doesn't matter
I have to go. I'm the one who can grow something.
I have to go.
Fuck.

Bryan instinctively hugs her, wraps her in his arms. She completely relaxes, hugs him back. They both stand in the embrace, Cassie drinking it in like water from a well. She hasn't been held in a very long time. Bryan starts to feel things shift and breaks away.

Bryan I should wash my hands –

Cassie tries to pull him back in, so Bryan fully separates himself. They stand staring at each other, Cassie feeling shaken by her desire for touch.

Cassie Sorry.

Bryan I –

Cassie I'm sorry. You're just
you're really easy to talk to.

The power goes out.

Bryan Shit.

Cassie Oh.

Bryan The generator. Hold on, I'm gonna go check it out.

Bryan exits. Cassie is alone in the dark.
    After a minute, she picks up her device to call Stella.
    Then Stella enters, wet and shivering.

Cassie Hey! Are you okay?

Stella Yeah, yeah, I went to the lake.
I just wanted to swim a little.

Cassie You got in?

Stella Power's out.

Cassie Yeah, it went out. Bryan's working on the generator.

Stella Okay.

Beat.

So that day, during the swim test –
    You're right.
    The testing us side by side . . . I was so tired. I hadn't
been able to sleep. I had this fear that I couldn't really name
– It would just be one and it was going to be you. And you
were swimming faster than me, you were swimming so
much faster than me. I knew you were so far ahead of me
and I didn't even think you wanted it, I knew you didn't
really even want it. And everything just went black . . .
    Lieutenant said your father would still be so proud of you
    and I thought no he wouldn't. He wouldn't . . .
    He would be proud of Cassie.

Cassie He would be proud –

Stella No. He wouldn't.
    When I found out I was pregnant –
    I had this peace, like I thought –
    I thought oh maybe this is what I'm meant to do
    since I guess I wasn't meant to do
    the thing I wanted to do
    And since I guess it's not? I've just been . . .
    I want this to be who I'm supposed to be
    out here, with Bryan
    but I don't know if it is?
    I want it to be?

They are quiet for a moment.

I realized
    I haven't even asked you
    What did it look like? Up there? Was it like Dad said?
    Was it beautiful?

72

Cassie nods.

I'm sorry
   I guess I always thought . . .
   if it could just be one, I thought it would be me.
   I wanted it to be me.
   I haven't known how to love you through this.
   But I want to, and . . .
   I know the tests are important.

Cassie Stella

Stella No, I've been angry, but that doesn't mean
   I shouldn't contribute. I can still contribute.

Cassie steps toward Stella, takes her hands.

Cassie You have so much to contribute. So much. You
don't have to make a decision right now.

Stella I want to do the tests.

Cassie Okay. Okay, I mean we can talk about it
tomorrow –

Stella No. I've decided. I'll come back with you.

Transition.

Act Four

The rain has stopped but lights are still out. Maybe one candle still going.

  Cassie is trying to sleep on the couch. Bryan comes in from working on the generator.

Cassie Hey. You're still up.

Bryan Trying to get it to work. Stella usually fixes it. I couldn't sleep.

Cassie I could try.

Bryan No it's okay. We should just wait it out.

Cassie I mean, I am an astronaut.

  Bryan can't help but laugh.

Bryan Let's just wait till morning. It's ancient, I should get it replaced.

  Beat.

Cassie Want to sit?

Bryan No, I'm gonna – go back to bed.

Cassie Can we talk? Let's sit outside.

Bryan (*after a moment*) Yeah.

  Bryan goes outside with her. Outside, it's quiet. Post-storm tranquility.

I guess I thought I knew what she wanted.

Cassie I get that. That's kind of how I felt. When I got out here. It's so different from everything she's known.

Bryan I just feel like she hasn't told me any of this, she hasn't wanted to go back, she's acted so hurt by the whole thing, and I've been trying to be there for her and I've spent this whole year trying to get her to be open with me, it's just so –

He is so upset he can't really finish his thought. Cassie reaches out and touches his shoulder, or hands. Bryan pulls away.

Cassie I'm . . .

Bryan I can't.

Cassie It's . . . No, yeah, I know.

Bryan Because you are easy to talk to. For me. You're open.

Cassie Yeah, well . . . I'm usually not. So.

Silence. Cassie and Bryan wrestle with the moment. Cassie breaks it, a little angry.

The truth is, I think she's been living out here with no purpose in her life, someone like her, someone as brilliant as her, as ambitious, that's got to have weighed on her.

Bryan No . . . purpose?

Cassie She's been trying to live this life, out here, away from it, but in the end, she's meant to be with us. She's meant to be back at work. So of course she was eventually going to come to this decision.

Bryan Actually Cassie we were doing really great, really great until you came out here. Then you get out here, and this happens.

A light in the back of the cabin turns on and maybe a small light in the kitchen, not enough for either of them to notice. Maybe the audience don't notice it.

Cassie You know that she and John were together for eight years?

75

Bryan What?

Cassie They met in undergrad, they were best friends,
    he wanted to marry her –
    she always said she would never get married –
    they worked on the same projects
    their lives were completely intertwined
    and then this happened, and she –

Bryan Why are you telling me this?

Cassie I'm just saying
    are you sure you're not like
    a band-aid for her?

Bryan What?

Cassie Just a way for her to cover up her pain for a while?
    Cover up her pain while she gets over it, gets over it
enough to come back to us.
    She said to me that even now that she's with you, now
that she changed her life, if she were given the opportunity
to go, she would.

Bryan . . . to Mars?

Cassie Yes.

Bryan . . . Well she's not going to.

Cassie But she would. Which shows me that she still wants
this. That coming back is what she wants.

Bryan You know what? Fuck this, I don't want to know
stuff like this, I only want to know the parts of her past that
she wants to share with me, I don't want to know all
this . . . shit –

Cassie Or do you? Does it change things?

Bryan You know what? I think you are really looking to
blow up your life because you're about to do a thing you

don't think is the right thing for you to do. And so you're looking to do something that will really fuck it up.

Do you need someone to tell you not to go?

Because shit I'll tell you not to go. Don't go.

I don't believe in going up there.

I do believe that you are incredible

and you will find someone HERE

who thinks that too and who

who can be with you

If that's what you want.

If you need someone to say that to you, to tell you not to go,

let me be that person.

Don't go, Cassie. Say no. Stay here.

She reaches for him and holds his face in her hands. He lets her, for a moment.

    Stella turns another light on.

    They break apart.

    No one says anything.

Stella I, uh – I fixed the generator.

I got up, I realized all the food was really going to go bad if I didn't.

Cassie Stella –

Stella I heard what you said.

Cassie I didn't mean –

Stella It was extremely convenient for me to be with John. It would have been hard to leave him any other way.

Bryan's not a band-aid.

I told you, I wanted to raise a human with him.

This is a valid way to live, I want this.

I can't believe you would say that, why would you even say that?

What are you trying to do?

Cassie I'm sorry. I wasn't doing anything, I was just trying to make him understand you.

Beat.

Stella (*a decision*) I think you should go tonight.

Cassie What?

Stella Yeah . . . I think . . . you'd better go.

Bryan Stella.

Cassie No, but you're –

Stella No, no. I'm not going to come.

Beat.

Cassie No, you have to come
You said you would come.

Stella Here, where's your stuff?

Cassie Why don't we just talk about this in the morning.

Stella Here's your bag.

Cassie I'm sorry, I didn't mean to hurt you, I was being an idiot –

Stella Can I not have anything? Why do you have to try to take EVERYTHING?

Cassie I would never try to take –

Stella Cassie I am really sorry, but this can't – I can't have you in my life. This is why. It's too much, it's too far, we can't exist together. You take things. You can't just let me be. I wish – I wish it could be different.

Cassie I can make this right. I won't go. I won't accept the mission. I can come live here, we can just be and garden and talk –

Stella No. Are you hearing me? You won't have a home with me. You won't have a place in my life.

Cassie Nothing happened! It was just a stupid / moment that I –

Bryan It / wasn't –

Stella It isn't about that, it's not about Bryan. It's about us.

Stella takes the manila envelope and tosses it on the table.

You need to go.

Cassie You are coming with me, let's talk about this.

Stella No, tell them sorry, they don't always get what they want, they can't have me back, too late.

Cassie Lella, they didn't want you!

The words hang in the air.

I wanted you!
   I fought for you!
   I have fought for you all year long,
   I asked them to write up the offer,
   so they did,
   but they don't need you.
   They are going to send me
   no matter what.
   I grew something in the ground.
   (*Desperate.*) You know that, right?
   I grew something
   You saw that I grew something?

Stella Yeah I know

Cassie Well why haven't you said anything?
   You haven't said anything.

Stella I didn't know what to say

Cassie You could have said good job
   Congratulations
   Something

Stella Sorry you don't have Dad to say that to you

Cassie I don't want Dad to say it, I never wanted Dad to
say it, I wanted you. I wanted YOU.
   I'm the one who wanted you to come back
   I'm the one who suggested the experiment
   Of course they want an experiment
   they want to learn
   but
   they have your blood
   they have your bone marrow
   they have your design
   they have what they need.
   I wanted you. I demanded you.
   All year I've been telling them
   They need to find a way to have you back
   and once I had the breakthrough
   once they offered me the mission
   I said
   The only way I'll go is if I have you.

Stella You can't have me. This is the thing. You can't have
me.

Cassie Who have you become? Who are you?!

Stella I'm your sister.

Cassie I'm YOUR sister. I'm your sister.
   (*At a loss.*) I'm sorry.

Stella What the fuck are you sorry for?
   They don't need me, yeah, great, I know.
   They told me that last time.
   I don't need to hear it again.

Stella throws Cassie's bag at the door. They all look at it for a moment, taking in what's happened.

Cassie I don't want this to be how it ends.
I'm sorry.

Stella Just go.

Cassie I love you – so much.

Stella brings her in for the quickest, roughest of embraces. Then she practically pushes her out the door.

Stella I love you too.
Go.

Cassie goes. Stella and Bryan are quiet. Stella shakes and sits down. Long, long silence. Eventually:

Bryan I'm sorry.

Stella No it's . . . It's okay.
It's okay.

Beat.
Bryan goes to her. Stella puts up a hand – she needs space.
Beat.

Sorry. I never should have asked her to come.

Bryan I think it's good that you did.

Stella This isn't good.

Bryan (*carefully*) I hope you don't think something happened. Nothing happened.

Stella I heard what you said but then you were holding her hands.

Bryan I was taking them away.

Stella nods. A moment.

Stella It's almost worse that she would try to make you think I don't love you. When she doesn't know. She doesn't know anything.

Bryan She doesn't?

Stella No.

Bryan I'm not a band-aid?

Stella . . . No.

Bryan Are you sure?

Stella I think at first . . . maybe it was something like that. Like maybe I felt so good around you because I was just hurting so much. You were like this oasis of goodness. But being around her made me realize how solid I've actually felt with you. Living this way. Appreciating moments and nature . . . and loving.

(*Processing.*) And even if they don't want me . . . they're going to use my design. Something I made, you know?

Bryan It's amazing. It really is.

Stella (*mind in a thousand places, trying to navigate through each different thought*) So I have contributed . . . I've already contributed . . .

(*Makes some sort of guttural sound.*) I hate her.

. . .

I'm going to miss her.

. . .

Going up, being an astronaut, it was all I ever wanted, you know? I couldn't imagine ever wanting anything else. It was the picture I would hold in my mind. When I swam, when I trained; in school, when I studied for exams, for so long I thought . . . all this will be worth it. To see the Earth from up there. To see stars. To walk on the Moon.

Bryan I want to know all that. You don't have to be afraid to tell me that.

Stella I think it's scared me. Wanting something else. And it hurts. It really hurts.

Beat.
Stella grabs his arms, pulls him to her, holds his face in her hands. A choice made. Maybe he kisses her, maybe they simply hold each other's gaze.

Bryan I don't want it to hurt.

Transition.

Act Five

A transition that shows almost a year passing. Stars move, the sun rises and falls, clouds pass. Everything gets a little darker and hotter. Hazier.

    Eleven and a half months later.

    Cassie is on one side of the stage. Stella is on the other side, standing or in a chair. They are not in the same room for the following conversation, but the scene could be played as if they are. They could look at each other at times, or the whole time, or not. The scene could include projections or be entirely projections, or not.

    Lights come up on both at the same time.

Cassie Hello?

Stella Cassie?

Cassie Hi.

Stella Hi.
  Can you hear me?

Cassie I can hear you. Can you hear me?

Stella Yes.
  Are you okay?

Cassie I don't know.

Stella What's wrong?

Cassie Thank you.

Stella What?

Cassie For speaking to me.

Stella Of course. I should have reached out sooner. You leave in three days, right?

Cassie Uh. Yeah.

Stella Are you okay?

Cassie I don't want to go.

Stella Come on, yes you do.

Cassie No. I don't. I don't think I can go.

Stella Do you want me to call someone for you? Someone to come talk to you?

Cassie NO. I just want to talk to you.

Stella Okay. Are you sure? Because this is a big deal if you're feeling this way –

Cassie Please. Let me talk to *you*.

Stella Okay.
Tell me – what you're feeling.

Cassie It's really good to see you. See your face.

Stella What?

Cassie What?

Stella Sorry I can't / hear you –

Cassie Oh okay. Can you hear me?

Stella Yes. Now I can.

Cassie I said it's good.
To see your face.

Stella Oh. Yeah. You too.
I should have come. To see you.

Beat.

But so . . . what's wrong? What are you afraid of? The
journey? The launch? Or – ?

Cassie I've just been thinking – I'm going to sound really
stupid, okay?

Stella Okay.

Cassie I've been thinking about forever.

Stella Forever?

Cassie Infinity. Endlessness.
How
I'm about to do a thing
that will be forever.
I will go there
and I will die there
and
it's just endless, the universe it's . . .
I've also been watching the feed from Mars, just the past
week or so, been watching it before I go to sleep, and Lella
there is nothing there. There's nothing. It's just desert. It's
dust. I keep trying to see beauty in it, or hope, or potential,
and all I see is dust and nothingness. And I *know* it's about
something bigger – but I can't help but look at where I'm
going and just see *nothing*.

Stella Yeah.
(*Considers.*) I've always thought the desert of it –
there's beauty in the nothing there.
It's beautiful because there's nothing. It's a place to start
over. It's a place where we haven't committed acts of
genocide against each other. There's been no pain there. No
wars. No greed. No murder. There are no gods, no men to
rule us, no animals to kill. No history of – hurting one
another.

Cassie Yeah.

Stella We've really messed this one up. And you get to be the one, to move us forward, to go to the next place, to give us the opportunity to try again.

Cassie But do you even believe that anymore? What about the Earth Advocates? What about the protests?

Stella I think we should be saving this planet. And I will be a part of the movement to save it. Yes.
  (*Difficult to say.*) And I don't know if we can. I don't know.

Cassie So maybe I should stay –

Stella I believe we should save this planet, *and* it has to be you. Think of all the hundreds of thousands of things that had to go right for you to be in this position right now: you had to take to it all so well, you had to work so hard, your body had to be exactly right, your mind had to be so strong, and all those things occurred. And you can grow something from nothing. You are the one who can do that.

Cassie Well none of this would have happened without you. / I would have never –

Stella No. Cassie. It's you. You must claim that for yourself. It's you.

  Beat.

Cassie, I'm . . . I'm going to have a baby.

Cassie . . . What?

Stella I'm going to have –

Cassie Sorry I can't hear / anything –

Stella Oh, okay.

  Silence.

Cassie?

Cassie Yeah.
   I can hear you.

Stella Bryan and I. We're going to have a baby.

Cassie Oh.

Stella I didn't know how to tell you, or if I should tell you.
   That's also why I haven't come. To say goodbye.

Cassie Wow.

Stella But I wanted to tell you.

   Beat.

Cassie?

Cassie I'm really happy for you.

Stella Thank you.
   Should I not have told you?

Cassie I don't know.
   If I go, I won't . . .

Stella You'll be able to speak to her.

Cassie On a screen.

Stella I know.

Cassie Oh my god I want to know her.
   Would I? Know her? If I stayed?

   Beat.

Stella I think so.

Cassie Yeah?

Stella Yes.

   Beat.

Cassie How can I go, knowing she'll be here?

Stella You should go *for her*.
   Maybe someday . . . she'll join you?
   (*Laughing.*) I don't know. Who knows. I don't know
what I'm doing.
   I don't know why I am bringing a baby into this horrible,
horrible world.
   I am trying to think of her as a new planet.
   Another place with no pain yet, no hurt.
   I have always thought it was awful and that the hope is
out there, way, way out there, but now my hope is right
here. And will be out there as well. With you.

Cassie It's not fair. I wish she was here already.

Stella I think it would be even harder.

Cassie How does it feel?

Stella Strange. Very strange.
   But it feels special.
   And right.

   A long look between them.

So.
   Are you going to go?

   Blackout
      End of play.